Contemporary
JOGGING

Jim Ferstle

cbi Contemporary Books, Inc.
Chicago

Library of Congress Cataloging in Publication Data

Ferstle, Jim.
    Contemporary jogging.

    Includes index.
    1. Jogging.   I. Title.
GV494.F47   1978   796.4′26   77-91153
ISBN 0-8092-7554-6
ISBN 0-8092-7575-9 pbk.

Published by Contemporary Books, Inc.
180 North Michigan Avenue, Chicago, Illinois 60601
Manufactured in the United States of America
Library of Congress Catalog Card Number: 77-91153
International Standard Book Number: 0-8092-7554-6 (cloth)
                                    0-8092-7575-9 (paper)

Published simultaneously in Canada by
Beaverbooks
953 Dillingham Road
Pickering, Ontario L1W 1Z7
Canada

Contents

Introduction

I received a letter the other day from a running coach. At the top of the letterhead were the accomplishments of his teams. At the bottom was the phrase "The Sport of the Gods."

I'm not going to tell you that jogging is quite that lofty, but an estimated ten million people are now engaged in it in the United States alone. Jogging no longer suffers from the bias that resulted in its name being associated with a painful, taxing experience.

Jogging was just a descriptive term used by writers to delineate the difference between the "real athletes" and the weekend athlete. The "real athletes" were smooth, powerful "runners." The weekend athlete was a slow, plodding "jogger."

The runners won medals and trophies. The jogger was satisfied with a T-shirt. As the number of people involved in jogging increased, however, it was the number of joggers that multiplied much faster than the number of runners.

Arithmetically it makes sense. There can be only one winner in a race. There are only so many runners able to contest for the top prize. The rest are in the race for different reasons. They have their own form of winning. It may be just to finish, or it may be to break a specific time barrier. It may be that they enjoy running and meeting other people. The race is as much a social occasion as it is a competitive event. Whatever the motivation, more and more people are running races and even more are just jogging for fitness.

These numbers have not gone unnoticed by shoe manufacturers or clothing retailers. Numbers mean a market for their products, and the jogger, not the runner, has been the primary target of their advertising. As a result, the image of the jogger has improved dramatically.

The jogger is no longer that sweaty, obese individual huffing and puffing along your block. Instead, the jogger is now dressed in the latest nylon shorts and singlet, with flared-heeled and waffle-soled shoes. "Dressed to kill," the form hasn't changed, but the image has.

This book will not attempt to tell you how to improve your image through your wardrobe. Instead, we'll try to help you improve your style. There'll be tips on how to start your program and how to maintain it or move up into racing, if that is your goal.

There will be information on diet, injuries, colds, how to correct flaws in your technique, how to dress to beat the cold and heat, and more. This book attempts to give you both a mental and a physical analysis of your exercise program.

It has material for joggers at all levels, from beginner to experienced. Pick out what interests you and adapt it to your program. Jogging is an individual sport. You have to adjust the activity to fit into your life-style.

One thing I strongly recommend is a checkup and/or "stress test." It sounds like a needless exercise, but it can give you a lot of useful information, as well as prevent a lot of trauma. If you do have any physical problems, the test will make you aware of your limitations.

If you are fit, it will give you a reading on your level of fitness and information you can build on for the future. Many colleges have physiology departments that are researching the effects of exercise and would be very interested in recruiting people for their studies.

For your investment of time you will reap the benefits of increased information on your physical progress in your jogging program. You will also be helping others by adding to the bank of knowledge being established for "joggers" as well as "runners."

Take the time to find a program like this or a doctor who is interested in the field. It will be well worth your effort.

Photo by Jim Ferstle

1

Getting started

Start slowly

A jogging program adds stress to your daily routine in an attempt to enable your body to adapt and increase your endurance. If you are beginning an exercise program with a very low level of fitness or you overdo your amount of exercise, you are going to have stiff and/or sore muscles. There will be times when jogging will be quite uncomfortable.

This is not exactly starting on a high note. But you should be aware of what obstacles you will encounter when you begin an exercise program. The first is the most important. Don't feel you have to do everything all at once. Improving your condition means adjusting your life-style to include exercise.

If you have to start by walking instead of jogging, do it. It's worth the extra time it takes and will start you off in the right frame of mind. Jogging or exercise doesn't have to be painful to be good for you. You don't have to go at full speed to get in shape. You're exercising to raise the potential within your body to a higher level, not to see how far you can push your body before it breaks down.

Many of us don't have the patience to use this type of approach. We start right away with heavy activity on the first day of our exercise program. The old rules of athletics die hard. The macho image of the athlete driving through pain barriers is the model we remember.

In reality, stiff and sore muscles are our immediate reward for ignoring our body's signals to ease into exercise. If you have a particularly strong will and tolerance for pain, you'll "gut it out" in the grand old tradition and end up limping from a torn muscle. All your dreams of physical fitness are crushed by the fact that you can't even walk properly, let alone run. You blame the activity, instead of your own stupidity. "Why did I ever try this crummy sport?" you ask yourself.

If you don't want to end your running career like this, there are plenty of ways to avoid it. Use common sense. If you put too much weight on the legs of a chair, they break. If you put too much stress on your legs, they start to break, too. Take your time. Plan your exercise program. Don't rush into it without thinking. If you are a sedentary individual, three things should be present before you begin your conditioning program.

The first is a desire to follow through on the activity. Set aside a half hour of your day for exercise. Fit it into your daily schedule. In the beginning it is necessary to fit your exercise program firmly into your everyday routine. There will be many times when you will think of better things to do. Starting the program is always the hardest part, and you need that desire to continue the activity to get you over the rough spots, when temptation calls for pleasure and jogging seems like pain.

The second ingredient is tied to the first. Know what to

expect and plan for it. Determine your strengths and weaknesses. Work on the weak parts and polish the strengths. For example, you may be very active before you start jogging, biking or swimming regularly. This will give you strengths of good muscle tone in certain muscles and a good cardiovascular system. Your weaknesses will be that the new muscles you use in jogging will be sore and there will be an imbalance between the strong muscles used in your other activity and the weak ones used in jogging.

The third part blends in here: set a realistic goal and work toward achieving it. Your goal in the case mentioned above would be to strengthen your legs to the point where you no longer have pain. You would work on stretching exercises to keep the muscles from tightening up, and on your running form to be sure the strong muscles don't dominate the weak ones and cause flaws in your technique.

Once you've achieved that goal, set another. It is much easier to maintain a program when you have clear goals. If there is no reason for you to fit your run into your daily routine, it will be easy to eliminate. If you have a goal that requires the daily jog, then you will have the incentive to keep at it until the jogging itself becomes an enjoyable enough portion of your day to be its own reward.

Most people jog too fast. A good rule to follow is if you can't talk while you're running, you're going too fast. Another guide is your pulse rate since it acts as a guide to the intensity of effort. There is a mathematical formula that can serve as an indicator for joggers who want to know how hard they should run to get the maximum benefit.

Take your resting heart rate and add to it .6 times the difference between your resting pulse rate and your maximum pulse rate. Your resting pulse rate should be taken when you get up in the morning or after you've been inactive. The maximum rate is 200 for 21-year-olds, with a subtraction of a beat a year for every year over 21.

If this formula is too complicated, an easier way to get

an approximation for a running heart rate is to double your resting pulse rate.

A good measure of how hard you ran is how soon your pulse returns to near normal after exercise. After you've showered and recuperated from your run, take a pulse check. If your pulse rate still hasn't come down significantly, you ran too hard. The pulse drops very quickly during the first three minutes after you stop running. Then it levels off and gradually returns to normal. Check your pulse before you run and for the first five minutes after you run. As you get in shape, your pulse will drop faster after exercise. Take the pulse again in about an hour. This will tell you if your run was too hard.

The maximum heart rate is about 200 at age 21, after which it goes down by about one beat per year. The formula for figuring your running or exercise pulse rate with the normal heart rate of 72 plugged in is: $72 + [.6 + (200-72)]$. (To take the pulse, always use your fingers, not the thumb. The thumb has a pulse of its own and can give you a double beat.

CHART FROM STRESS TEST FOR JOGGERS

RX FOR JOGGERS

Age	Maximum pulse/ heartbeat rate	85%
22	198	168
24	196	166
26	194	164
28	192	163
30	190	161
32	189	160
34	187	158
36	186	158
38	184	156
40	182	154
45	179	152
50	175	148
55	171	145

Here a runner takes his
pulse on the neck. You can
also take it on your wrist

The best place to find a pulse is on the neck near the base of
your jaw or on the thumb side of your wrist.)

Warm-up

Begin your exercise session with a warm-up. A warm-up is just like its name; you warm your muscles through gentle exercise and stretching. This can be done by easy jogging, walking, and stretching. Muscles stretch easier and contract faster when they are warm.

The intent of this activity is to help prevent injury from any sudden motion or twisting. If the muscles are limber, they are less likely to snap under pressure. When you do your stretching, do it slowly. No jerky motions, no bouncing up and down, which only causes tension. You're treating your muscles like rubber bands, pulling them out and letting them snap back. As the muscle is being snapped back and forth, it tries to stretch and contract at the same time. The result is a push and pull action that could cause a muscle tear.

Don't stretch past the point where you feel pain. If you are bent over to touch your toes and feel pain when your hands are almost there, stop. Slowly straighten up and try the stretch again. If you feel tight at the same point or before that point, stop that exercise and move to another. If, however, you are able to stretch farther without pain, go as far as you can and then straighten up and try again. Sometimes muscles have more tension than usual and require more gentle stretching to loosen them. Take your time and do the stretches slowly and gently.

Learn to listen to your body. Stiffness and soreness are the body's messages to go slowly and gently. Heed the message and you will stay healthy. Ignore the warning and be prepared for the consequences.

Generally, running is a pretty spontaneous activity. From day to day, minute to minute, you can change how fast you run, how far, and where. Successful runners monitor their bodies for signs of how they are adapting to stress and plan their runs accordingly.

Keeping a record

One easy way for you to both learn about your system and keep a record of your progress is a training diary. Training diaries come in many forms, but the essential information for your daily log is your resting pulse rate, your weight, the number of hours of sleep for the day, how many times and how far you ran, and a short notation of how you felt during the day. Sample daily log sheets can be found on pages 8 and 10.

This diary has many advantages that make it worth the small amount of time required each day to take the measurements and write them down. Once you get into a pattern of running every day, four times a week, or whatever, keep it. Your body runs in cycles with a definite rhythm. Once you establish this rhythm, you should maintain it. Changes only upset the system and force it to make other adjustments besides the one it is making for the exercise itself. A diary monitors that rhythm. The pulse rate gives you an indication of the strength of your heart and your cardiovascular fitness. If you check your pulse every morning when you wake, you will have not only an accurate indicator of your condition but a test of your general health as well.

Your heart rate will go down as your condition improves, but there should not be a big difference in your pulse rate from day to day. If your pulse is ten beats or more higher than it was when you took it the day before, your body is giving you a message. Your resistance is low and you are tired or your body is fighting a virus. Your body is telling you that it needs more rest. Be careful to take your pulse at the same time every day. This doesn't mean the same clock hour, just during the same cycle; for example, when you get up in the morning or when you are ready for bed at night. This applies to your weight also.

Do your weighing in the nude for best results, not because the scale responds more to an unclothed body but because it is the most consistent. You don't have the extra weight of clothes to alter your weight measurement.

Weight loss during exercise is a good indicator of the severity of the workout. On a hot day a heavy workout may cause your body weight to drop five to eight pounds. You should weigh yourself before and after workouts for a while to determine your average weight loss; also, before and after meals to see how much you put back through eating and drinking.

Rapid weight loss can also indicate problems in your system. It is not healthy to lose big chunks of anything. The body must adapt to any loss, and while it helps to lose unneeded fat, too much too soon causes problems.

Daily Training Log

Date 7/19/71
Weather Cool-Warm-Rain

A.M.
Weight _____ Pulse 39?

Workout 4mi @ 7mp — 1mi Warmup 1mi
II 5:30 3mi

Training area Rds.

P.M.
Workout 1mi int. 110's(16) 18-14sec. first 8 pr 140-160 $^{18-16}$
last 8 $^{15-14}$ 160-170 7mi Rds. + Woods

Training area Grass - Rds. - Woods

Resistance workout _____ Swimming

Physical attitude Sore in upper right leg-tired pushed mile and 110's

Mental attitude Fair not high but adequate better than usual on intervals - concentrated on pulse rate.

Personal comments and observations _____

Mileage: 9 a.m. 11 p.m. — other 20 total 20 accumulative

Meet result/performances II 1st 5:30 @ 1mi hills

Date 7/20/71
Weather Cool

A.M.
Weight _____ Pulse 43

Workout 4mi — 6mi fartlek trails

Training area Rds. Trails

P.M.
Workout 6 mi — 3mi

Training Area Rds.

Resistance workout Swimming

Physical attitude Sore in the legs esp. Hamstrings Hard to get started

Mental attitude Poor didn't enjoy it at all - didn't even want to run—just bored.

Personal comments and observations _____

Mileage: 10 a.m. 9 p.m. — other 19 total 39 accumulative

Meet result/performances _____

Moderation is the key word even when it comes to sleep. Every person needs a certain amount of sleep to stay healthy. Your diary can give you an accurate picture of the amount of rest you need. If you get too much, you may feel sluggish. If you get too little, you feel flat and listless.

The diary is a valuable tool. You shouldn't try to depend on your memory. It is much better to have something written down to jar it. For a racer, the diary tells what training patterns work best and how to mix rest with stress to produce a peak performance. If you are the average runner or jogger, the diary keeps a record of your progress. It gives you a breakdown of how you met or failed to attain your goals. It helps you keep going on a weight-reduction program by showing you the results of your exercise in weight loss. It gives you a tool for planning your program and meeting your goals.

The jogger is not treading the fine line between injury and maximum performance like the racer reaching a peak. The performance that concerns the jogger is the daily routine, what effect it is having on the system, and how to best utilize that effect to achieve the goals of the individual program.

Make it interesting

If you find yourself getting bored, run with a friend; it will take your mind off your own running and add the camaraderie of another individual. Don't get competitive, however, and try to run each other into the ground. Your aim is to enjoy the run together, not see who is the faster runner on that particular day.

If you need a change in scenery, find a different route. A change in scenery is not only a physical shift to a different terrain but is also food for your mental health. Try hilly courses as well as flat ones, golf courses, and forest trails. Running doesn't confine you; it liberates you to discover areas you can't get to on wheel.

Individual Training Schedule

Name _John Doe_   Month _July_   year _1973_

Date	Day	Sleep	Weight	Pulse	Workouts	Workout	Terrain	Distance	Comments
1	Mon	9	145	—	1	10 min @ 5½ mi	ISLAND ROAD	10	Very hard. Abductor too
2	Tues	9	—	50	2	4 mi / 6 mi	Courts Coast	10	Twist, sore
3	Wed	8	—	52	2	4 mi warmup 8×440(?) 110 jog 2 mi WD	Bruno	10	Very loose
4	Thurs	8.5	—	—	2	4 mi / 5 mi	15 RTE	12	Calf tight
5	Fri	8.5	—	—	2	4 mi / 6 mi	15 RTE	12	Calf still sore
6	Sat	8.5	—	—	2	4 mi / 6 mi (22.9)	OAKS PK	12	Everything stable
7	Sun	8.0	—	—	1	10 min	8	FIESTA IS	10 (26)	Tired - legs OK
8	M	8.0	145	—	2	4 mi 10 min fartlek (WD)	15 RTE	14	Dead - running OK later
9	Tu	8.0	—	48	2	5 min 10 min	CANAL	14	Tired, weak
10	W	6.5	—	—	2	4 min 2 min WORup 10K 33:16 2 min WD	BALBOA	14	Look strength
11	Th	7.0	—	—	2	4 min 10 min (WD)	15 RTE	14	Couldn't get going
12	Fri	7.5	—	47	2	6 min 10 min (WD)	15 RTE	16	Calves sore - tired
13	Sat	8.0	—	—	2	4 min 10 min (WD)	15 RTE	14 (WD)	Very easy
14	Sun	8.5	—	47	1	1½ hrs run	MISSION BAY	14	Tired - mild sprint
15	M	7.5	143	45	2	4 min 1×880 12×440 12 WD (WL)	FIESTA IS	15	Leg tired - no zip
16	Tu	8.5	145	49	2	4 min 10 min (WD)	15 OBS	14	Legs tired + tight
17	W	8.0	—	42	2	4 min 10 min (WD)	15 RTE	14	Legs sore but lively
18	Th	8.0	—	44	2	4 min 11 min (WD)	FIESTA IS	15	Very little stiffness
19	F	8.0	—	45	2	4 min 10 min (WD)	15 RTE	14	READY - running sore
20	Sat	7.5	—	44	1	2 min wormup 10K race 33:24 (8:15-16:06) 2 min jog 4 mi	Mission Bay	14	+ tight - Twist
21	Sun	8.0	143	45	2	14 min / 10 min (WL)		14 (WD)	At leg pace - bus, Twist
22	M	6.5	143	49	2	4 min 10 min	FIESTAK	14	Legs no soreness ex
23	Tu	6.5	146	42	2	4 min WUP 6×880(?) 440 J 2 mi WD	MISSION BAY	14	Strong stuff
24	W	8.5	—	42	2	10 min (WD)	FIESTA IS	14	Strong - legs fine
25	Th	8.0	—	45	2	4 min 10 min	15½ RTE	16	Both cool - only fair
26	F	8.0	—	50	2	4 min 10 min (WL)	FIESTA IS	14	
27	Sat	7.0	—	45	2	2 mi WR-up 1 mi 4:37 8 mi		14	Legs stiff 45 ex
28	Sun	8.0	—	47	2	4 min warmup 10K race 33:21 - 30 yd score birthday race 4 mi	FIESTA IS leg	14 (WD)	Legs stiff
29	M	8.0	145	45	2	10 min (WD)	FIESTA IS	14	Open legs - legs stable
30	Th	7.0	145	45	2	4 min 12×440 (J) 150 J WD	Mission Bay	15	Felt bad
31	W	8.0	145	48	2	4 min 10 min	FIESTA IS	14	Everything better
AVG.			145						

Total	419
Year	4,131
Life	27,281

You may want to time your runs to give yourself an incentive. You can set your own course records and race yourself for imaginary prizes. Don't get too carried away, however. Racing is for those who are prepared for it, not for everyone. Keep your "races" low key until you're ready to handle something more strenuous.

There may also be a time for you to run that is more favorable than others. Some of us are morning people, and others function best in the afternoon. According to studies, morning runners stick with their running longer but are injured more often. Evening runners quit in larger numbers but suffer fewer injuries. Find out what suits your system best.

These are all just mental tricks to add variety to your activity. They will help you get through the days when the weather is bad and you don't feel like running. They are aimed at decreasing boredom, but in reality jogging is only as boring as you make it.

Some people even experiment with their breathing. There is no right or wrong way to breathe. Take in as much oxygen as you can. If you can breathe through your ears, do it. The more oxygen, the better. The most important aspect in breathing is your posture. If you are erect in the upper body, you are giving the diaphragm plenty of room to expand and contract and the lungs also can expand to their fullest.

There are systems for breathing or maintaining a rhythm while you breathe. This focuses your attention on the subject but doesn't get more air into your system. Breathing is essentially an involuntary action that you can control up to a point. You can hold your breath for only so long before the body takes over and forces you to begin breathing again.

Be creative, your body is a complex instrument. Let your mind run wild with the possibilities for enjoying your physical fitness. The fitter you are, the more you will be able to do. That, in itself, should be enough motivation for you to keep active.

Photo by Jim Ferstle

2
Technique

The first question you often hear is: what is the proper form for running? Is there a special technique that will make you a good runner? What is the best way to run?

Natural movement

The answer is doing what comes naturally. The best "runners" to watch for tips on style are animals. They live on their feet and depend on their lower extremities a great deal more than man. The mother leopard doesn't take her baby cub aside one day and say, "Listen, son, it's time for you to run. You put the right paw under the . . . ." Movement comes naturally.

It does for man also, but we have a way of inhibiting our own natural motion. We wear shoes with heels that restrict the stretching of our calf muscles. We drive around in cars and spend much of our time in motion on our posteriors. Our limbs become weak and imbalanced, and we lapse into incorrect forms of motion.

You see it every day on the street. The executive in a hurry to get to an important meeting is briskly striding through the crowd. The upper body is hunched forward, legs extended as far as they can reach. Each foot lands heavily on the heel, and the feet slap to the ground audibly. You can almost hear the shock waves travel up the person's leg with each slap of the shoe. The dasher is showing you everything not to do. Overstriding and exaggerated forward body lean are two of the mistakes this person makes in haste to get from place to place. He wastes energy and works up a good sweat.

A more fitting example of proper style would be a fashion model. The model's posture is very erect. If you tied a string to an ear and dropped it straight down, it would bisect the body into equal halves. The movement is economical. A slight lift of the knee on one leg and a push from the opposite foot as it rolls forward on the toes starts the motion. The lead leg lands softly on the outside edge of the foot, rolls

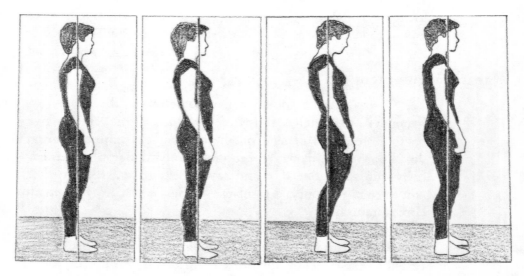

These illustrations show you the rights and wrongs in posture. The first stance is good posture, while each of the others strains certain portions of the body.

onto the ball of the foot, and pushes off. The other leg lifts from the knee and swings forward to repeat the motion. The arms sway gently at the side, and the upper body remains erect with no excess movement from side to side—a picture of economy in motion. All the effort is directed toward moving forward. Nothing is wasted. It is a style to emulate in your running.

The best way to reduce stress is to become more efficient. Your efficiency improves as you gain strength and endurance. That is the real difference between the jogger and the runner. The runner has more strength, endurance, and efficient motion and therefore looks and performs in a manner that is distinct in its style.

Discovering and developing a style

The entire stride is divided into two phases, the stance phase and the swing phase, of what is called the gait cycle. This cycle is similar in both running and walking. The primary differences occur in the contact stage of the stance phase. In walking and jogging the foot makes contact on the heel and the full foot. The runner does not land on the full foot but, rather, rolls onto the ball of the foot after landing lightly on the heel.

Many walkers can keep up with a slow jogger because the motion remains essentially the same. The same amount of propulsion is generated. In most cases, one foot is almost always on the ground, rather than both feet off the ground, as in a running stride.

This stage, known as the recovery phase when both feet are off the ground, is the result of the powerful thrust from the third stage of the cycle, the propulsion stage. When a runner is moving at top speed, heel contact is minimal. A sprinter runs on the balls of the feet, and the heels seldom touch the ground. These high-speed gaits cannot be maintained for an extended period of time.

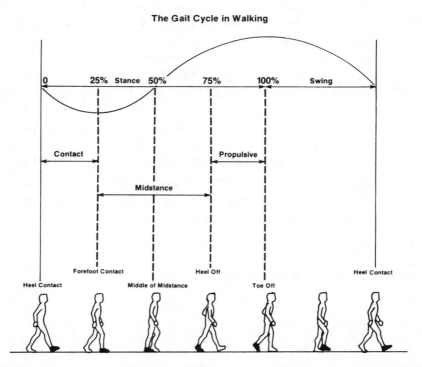

The Gait Cycle in Walking

This is the breakdown of your walk into segments of what is called the gait cycle. It has two phases, the stance phase and the swing phase. In these phases one makes contact, is supported by at least one foot in mid-stance, and is propelled by that foot forward to make contact with the other foot.

If you want to examine your style, just test it out by walking. What you are doing through this method is using a sort of instant replay/stop action capacity to mirror how you would look while running. Each movement has a purpose, and that purpose is to push you forward. Speed up your walk using the same motions you use in running and look at what you're doing.

Contrary to what you might think, running efficiency begins with the hips. Your pelvic area controls your lean and thereby much of your efficiency when running. If you are moving with your pelvis stuck out behind you, your upper

Comparison of Stance and Swing Phases of Gait

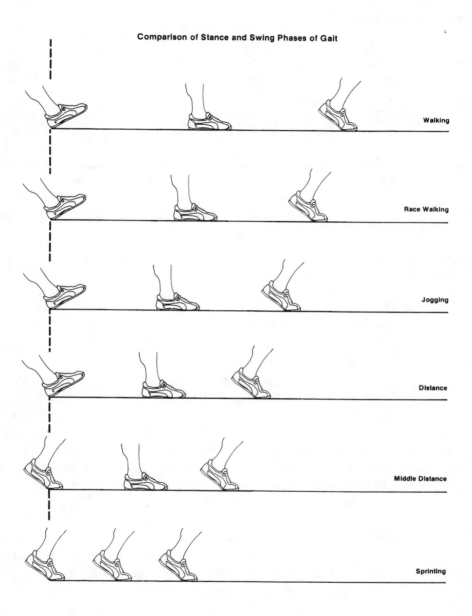

Walking

Race Walking

Jogging

Distance

Middle Distance

Sprinting

This illustrates the different contact points for the various gaits from walking to sprinting. It shows how foot contact varies as your speed and range of motion increase.

The Gait Cycle in Running

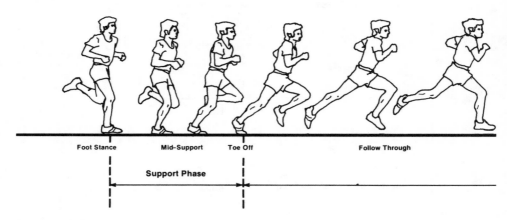

| Foot Stance | Mid-Support | Toe Off | Follow Through |

Support Phase

This is an example of the running gait cycle. It differs from walking and jogging because there is a period when both feet are off the ground.

body will be leaning forward. To move forward, your legs then have the added weight of your upper body to move upward before they can push the body forward.

If you have ever watched a sprinter come out of the crouched position at the starting line, or tried it yourself, you know how much effort it takes to get moving. The weight of the upper body and the center of gravity, which is located in your hips, are over the legs. Get down in a sprinter's start and try walking forward while you move your body upright. Notice how much work it takes to move in this position.

Stand with your feet flat on the ground and your back straight against the wall. Start to fall forward. Lift the knee of your right leg and stop your fall by landing on the ball of your right foot. Look at yourself. You're in the perfect accelerating position. Your weight is on the balls of your feet, your arms are pumping in rhythm with your legs, and your body is at about a 45 to 60-degree angle driving forward. Start walking while at the same time gradually lifting your body to an erect position. You are now in perfect form for running—eyes forward, head erect, and your body

Forward Swing   Foot Descent

Recovery Phase

straight up. The forward lean is used only when you are accelerating or changing from one speed to another. Slowly speed up your leg movement and increase the length of your stride. Lift the knees higher and start applying more force with your feet. You'll find you are breaking contact with the ground and are now running. That's all there is to it.

Not everybody runs like this, however. Some great runners have had the most unusual form. Their heads bobbed, and arms were tight against the body. One Olympic champion could not use one of his arms, while another had had a childhood bout with polio. Both overcame their handicaps to become champion runners.

Problems and cures

The most common form problems in joggers are easily diagnosed. Running on the toes, overstriding, hunched shoulders, tension, body rotation, and poor posture are all symptoms of bad form and can be corrected.

Running on the toes is one of the most common errors.

This illustrates the forces at work in the propulsion of the body forward in a running stride. The body is erect, with the center of gravity, located in the hips, in front of the foot as it pushes off the ground to drive the body forward. A represents the backward-downward thrust of the foot; B is the downward component of force A; and C is its backward component. D represents the reaction to force A that propels the body. E and F are the upward and forward components, respectively, of the propelling force.

Sprinters run on their toes, but they are moving at full speed with a long stride and have strong, well-conditioned legs. The jogger who runs on the toes resembles a kangaroo. The energy that is supposed to propel you forward pushes you upward and forward instead. To correct this, you just revert to your natural motion of heel to toe. Running on your toes is not a natural form of motion. You don't walk on your toes, and you won't run on your toes unless you've trained yourself to do it. Only sprinters are trained that way, and they can maintain that stride for only a short period of time.

Overstriding is another common error. You watch runners on television with long, flowing strides and try to emulate them. This doesn't work. You have to run within your limits, not try to copy someone else's form. One of the signs of overstriding is your view of the horizon as you run. It generally bobs up and down. The ground isn't jumping, you are. To cure this problem, you have to concentrate on using a quicker, shorter stride. Try running uphill. This will force you to take shorter strides, especially as you get tired. Fatigue is the danger in overstriding. Your muscles tire, and your stride shrinks. You begin to plod and land heavily on your heels. This is uncomfortable as well as exhausting.

To cure the overstriding completely, you may have to strengthen your legs. Running uphill will help do this. At first you will be able to maintain the quicker rate of movement of your legs for only short periods without tiring. Get comfortable with the shorter stride and concentrate on maintaining it. The general tendency is to go back to the long stride once you get tired. Fight the urge and maintain your short stride.

Get into a cadence and keep it. One good way is to run to music or a beat. If you have an earphone radio, you can wear it to take your mind off the way you are running and concentrate on the rhythm of the run. Long striders run with the rhythm of bum, bum, bum, bum, while the natural stride is more like a dot, dot, dot, dot.

If you find yourself swaying from side to side, the problem is most likely in your head or arms. Your head may be rolling from side to side or your arms swinging across your body. The head should remain stationary on top of your shoulders, with the arms relaxed at the side and bent from the elbow at about a 90-degree angle. The angle opens a little as they swing down and closes back to 90 degrees as they swing up.

When you have the correct posture and your head is erect, you will get a good view of the horizon. If you are getting a good view of the ground and not much else, you are leaning too far forward or your head is dipped forward. Like the arms, the chin should form about a 90-degree angle with the neck when it is in its proper position.

Keep relaxed. If you get tired and your whole body starts to sag, you have to concentrate hard to maintain correct posture. Don't tense up to do it. Keep the pelvis forward, the shoulders back, and the chin up. Maintain as little muscle tension as possible for maximum efficiency.

Once this form begins to break down and you hunch forward, you begin to notice it in your arms. They pull in close to your sides and form more of a 45-degree than a 90-degree angle. This will begin to rotate the body from side to side, waste energy, and tire you more quickly. Relax the arms and drop them to 90 degrees. Shrug the shoulders and stop and do some limbering-up exercises. Don't curl up into a ball.

Your hands will also give you signs of tension. If they are clenched in a fist or limp and flapping from the wrist, they are adding to the tension. They should be lightly closed and move as one with the forearm.

If you do have some of these faults in your running style, don't try to correct them all at once. Go after one at a time and correct that before moving on to the next. Chances are by curing one you will cure another at the same time. Since form is the first thing to deteriorate when fatigue sets in, concentrate on maintaining your form as you get tired. It will make the run much more pleasant.

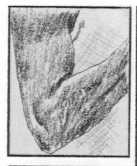

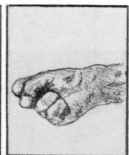
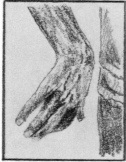

Correct running form is shown above. Common problems include (clockwise from bottom left) limp wrist, elbow at 90°, clinched fist, and arm across chest.

We've talked a lot about the upper body because this is the part you can control the most. The only real control that you have over your legs is the rate of speed and the amount of knee lift. The rest of the action happens so quickly that it is next to impossible to consciously control it.

If you have good posture and strong legs and feet, the rest of the running motion will fall into place. Use an erect posture and a short, efficient stride, roll from heel to toe, and relax. These are the basics. Follow them and you'll get the most out of your body and your exercise.

Photo by Anne Kelly

3
Getting in shape

You may be saying to yourself, "Why does he keep mentioning warm-up and warm down so much?" Because they are probably two of the keys to your enjoyment of jogging. With a proper warm-up and stretching, you can avoid much of the minor pain that inhibits your enjoyment of exercise.

Commitment

Warming up and warming down properly involves a mental as well as physical commitment. It forces you not only to listen to your body but also to approach your exercise in a controlled manner rather than dash into it without thinking. Most injuries suffered by runners are the result of a lack of adequate preparation.

You've had a rough day at work and have just enough time to get a run in before you have to get back and shower for an important dinner meeting. You rush out the door and gallop off into your run without thinking of how fast you're going. Your body is cold, your muscles are tense, and you are in a hurry. If you're not too tired or your muscles are flexible, you may get away with your transgressions without a problem. Many are not that lucky.

You ignore the little twinge in your right calf. You don't have time to stop, and so you run harder even though your body is telling you to slow down. You finish and rush into the shower. Still sweating, you towel off and dress for dinner. You rush off to the meal still hot and flushed from the run. You don't even notice that your leg is bothering you. You don't notice until you try to stand up after sitting at the dinner table. That leg is now stiff and sore and you've got a torn muscle. You feel stiff all over because you didn't take time to cool down after the run before jumping into the shower.

Have you learned your lesson? Probably not. You'll most likely do it again sometime, until one day when you really hurt yourself. Then you might start to incorporate a warm-up and a warm down in your runs. They don't have to be separate from the runs. Use the first portion of the distance you run to warm up the muscles and get them feeling loose. Use the final portion to wind back down.

The important thing to remember in the warm-up is to get your heart pumping blood into the system faster to meet the increased needs of your system. This will increase your body temperature and make the muscles warm and able to stretch and contract more easily.

At this point you are ready to perform the heavy portion of your exercise. After the strenuous part is completed, you should take the time to return the heart rate to normal and lower the body temperature. That is the essence of the warm down. It is like your car's choke valve. You put on the choke and run the engine to warm up the car so that it will run smoothly. When you get the car running and up to 55 mph, you don't back off the throttle right away. You gradually decrease your speed to let the car slow down gradually.

Do the same with your own engine, the heart. If you stop after a particularly hard run, where you were up to 180 or 200 beats per minute, and go right inside and shower

Exercises for Feet and Legs

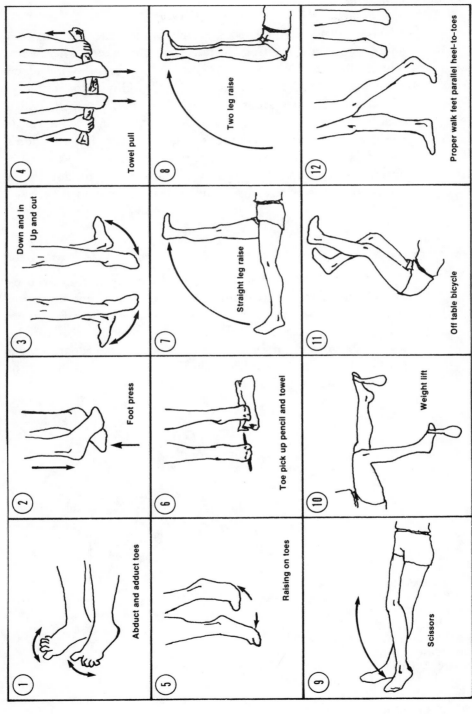

1. Abduct and adduct toes
2. Foot press
3. Down and in / Up and out
4. Towel pull
5. Raising on toes
6. Toe pick up pencil and towel
7. Straight leg raise
8. Two leg raise
9. Scissors
10. Weight lift
11. Off table bicycle
12. Proper walk feet parallel heel-to-toes

As with most exercise, start with your feet. Exercises 1, 2, 3, 5, 7, 8, 9, 11, and 12 can be done every day before you run. Exercises 4 and 6 are for people with sore shins and feet. Exercise 10 is to help prevent shin splints or to rehabilitate you if you've had them.

without some jogging or walking to let the system cool down, you are inviting serious consequences. The heart, which was pumping out the blood to meet the increased demands of the exercise, has been shut down too quickly. Blood stays in the areas where it has been pumped, and a condition known as blood pooling may occur. The result could be cramping, hyperventilation, or fainting. So don't shut down your system without first giving it time to warm down. The warm down will eliminate the lactic acid from your system as it pays back the oxygen debt you may have built up.

The warm-up

You will benefit from the development of a daily routine of stretching or flexibility exercises before and after you run. The important stretching is done after the run, unless you have very tight muscles before the run. Normally the warm-up will be sufficient to get your muscles prepared for a faster effort. The illustrations on pages 27-33 are examples of exercises you should do before the run.

Next stretch your calf muscles. This exercise is known as the wall push-up. You start by standing close to the wall and doing a "push-up" standing up. Gradually move away from the wall with your feet and repeat the push-up motion. You will end up stretching all the way up to your hamstring muscles in the upper leg.

To stretch the muscles on the inside of your legs, start by standing with your legs spread apart slightly. Lean over to one side, stretching one leg while bending at the knee with the other. Repeat the motion with your other leg.

To stretch your hamstring muscles, elevate your leg on or against the surface of a chair or a wall. Bend from the waist and try to touch your nose to your knee.

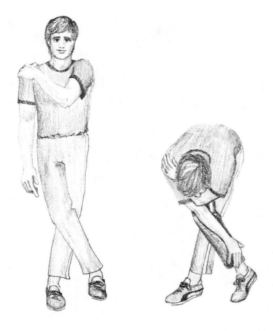

Another type of hamstring stretch doesn't involve the imbalance of keeping one foot off the ground. Stand straight and cross your legs. Bend down and touch your toes.

To make it simple, just do a regular toe-touch exercise. The chair exercise involves the muscles of your opposite leg; the crossed-leg toe touch stretches more than just your hamstring and calf muscles. This exercise is just a straight up-and-down motion and stretches only those muscles.

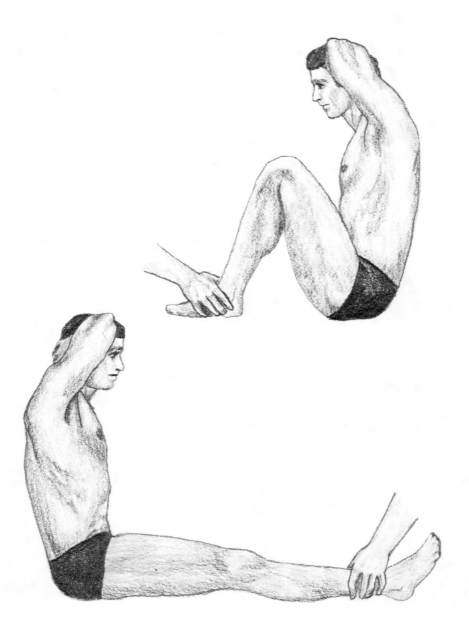

To exercise your stomach muscles, you can do sit-ups, either bent leg or straight leg.

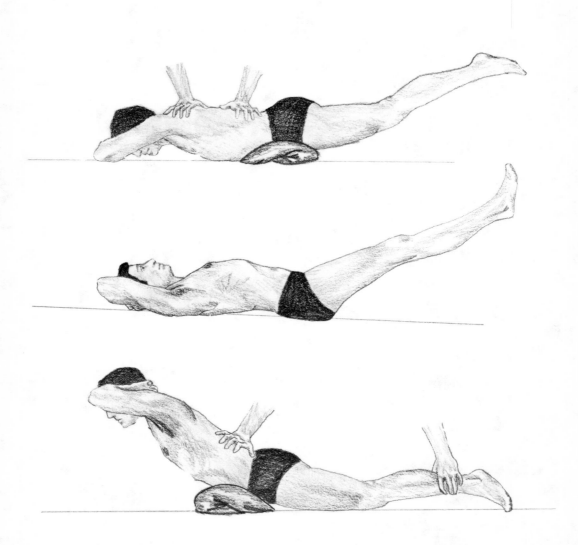

For your back, you can do a series of leg raises and trunk-raising exercises from a similar position.

All the foregoing exercises have a particular purpose. If you just want to do a quick set, here is an example of a group that will limber you up. Remember, however, no fast, jerky motions; do them slowly.

The warm down

Since most joggers are fairly fatigued at the end of a run, the stretches afterward are important for relaxing those tight muscles. When you are fatigued, you tend to shorten

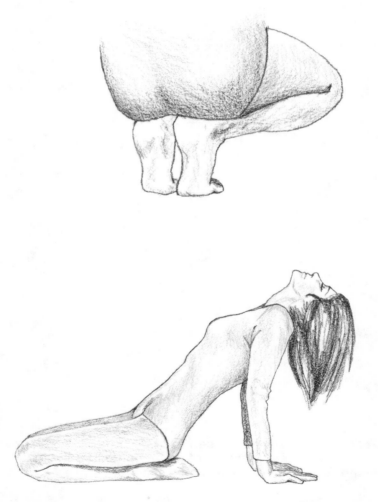

After your run, you may want some relaxing stretches to relieve tension. For the first exercise, squat down on your feet and raise the toes. Then lie on your legs with your feet straight back underneath you. Using your arms for balance, stretch your body back until you can touch your head to the ground behind you. This may hurt a little, so go slowly until you are used to it.

your stride and the whole body "shrinks" a little. Stretching afterward relaxes the muscles and helps prevent them from staying tight. The following illustrations are the types of stretches you should try after you run.

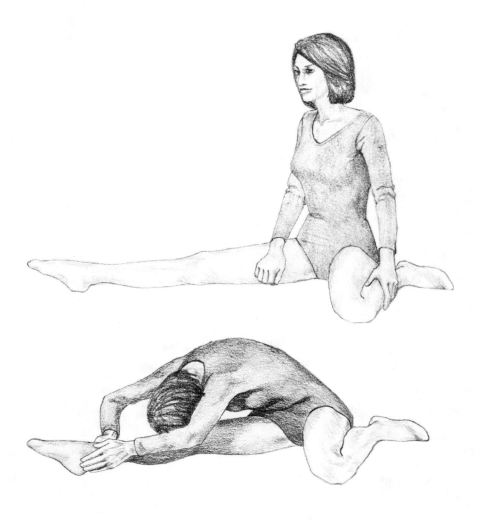

Next, do an exercise known as the hurdlers stretch, from the position a hurdler has while clearing the hurdle. Sit down with one leg straight out and the other bent at the knee and flat on the ground. Lean down from the waist and touch your nose to your knee. Straighten up to the sitting position again, then lean backward and touch your head to the ground as you did in the previous exercise.

While you're still in a sitting position, you can do one more stretch—a toe touch. Just bend from the waist and touch your toes with your hands. Bend a little farther and try to touch your knee with your nose.

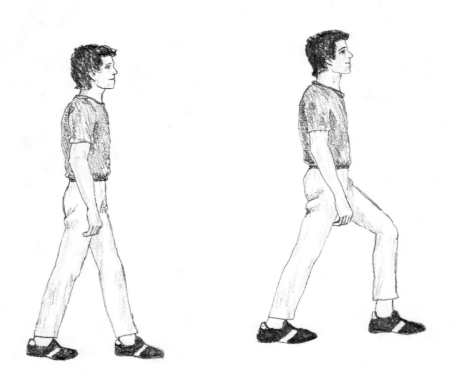

Now that you are standing, you can stretch your calf muscles. Just lean forward on one foot and stretch out with the back foot.

As a final exercise, you can touch your toes from a standing position.

Strengthening weak areas

There is also a series of preventive or rehabilitative exercises that may be useful if you encounter leg or foot problems. These exercises involve lifting weights as resistance for the muscles and stretching against a form of resistance. They are not, in the pure sense, stretching exercises, but they perform that function against resistance.

Knee extended

Heel Cord Stretch

Quadriceps Stretch

Towel

The Plow

Posterior Muscle Group Stretch

5 Lbs.

Knee extended

Straight Leg Raises for Knee Rehabilitation

Shin Strengthener

Quadriceps Strengthener

These exercises help strengthen weak muscles. They involve stretching against resistance and should be done with care. You generally use light weights and do many repetitions.

Photo by Jim Ferstle

4

Injuries and colds

If the runner has any enemies, they are injuries and colds, both of which hamper the enjoyment of the activity. They can usually be avoided through careful planning and restraint.

Types of injuries

There are two basic causes of injury. One is a direct trauma like a twisting motion that puts severe stress on a joint or a muscle. Your ankle, for example, is injured when you step in a hole and "twist" it. These are "freak" accidents that seem to haunt us every now and then. They do their damage immediately, being at their peak when they strike.

The second cause you have control over, sometimes even as to severity. This is overuse injury, a gradual accumulation of microtraumas. Stated simply, it means you overextend yourself. You try to do too much too soon, or you are not prepared for what you are doing. You might also have a weakness in your physical structure that causes added stress and, if not compensated for, injury. This imbalance is not noticed during normal daily activities but becomes a problem because of the added stress of an exercise program.

Most injuries follow a distinct pattern. The direct trauma injury hits you right away. The best cure is to avoid the situations that lead to it. Overuse injuries are usually the result of your own mistakes. Very rarely do you get a severe overuse injury that incapacitates you without warning. The first signal is stiffness and soreness in your muscles. Stiff muscles are tired muscles. Their flexibility goes first, and you have a more limited range of movement.

If you work hard on stiff muscles without stretching or warming them up, you move to the soreness stage. This is a microtrauma. You start damaging muscle tissue because it can't handle the increased pressure. If you keep pushing the sore muscle or joint, you are risking further damage. You should be able to exercise lightly but only after thoroughly warming up and stretching your muscles.

Handling injuries

You should soak the injured area in cold water or rub it with ice after exercise to prevent swelling and decrease any hemorrhaging that may occur. If you take it easy and rest the injured area, you will recover without losing your ability to run. You can exercise near your normal level, only not so fast or so intensely, without fear of further damage.

If you ignore the warning your body is giving you, you'll pay the price. The injury will move from a soreness that goes away after warming up to one that stays all through your exercise and increases in intensity. This type of injury may not limit your mobility, but it makes you painfully aware of the damaged tissue. It is a dull pain that throbs during and after exercise. You must decrease your running distance or speed if you wish to prevent further injury.

In many cases you can trace an injury back to a certain

form of activity or a structural problem. It may have happened during a fast run, a run uphill, or some other specific exercise. Your first option is to avoid the type of exercise that caused the injury. If this doesn't help, you haven't diagnosed the cause properly. It may be that you have a structural problem. For example, one leg may be shorter than the other, or you may have bad arches. If as the result of running too much, too fast, or on a particular surface, you get pains that you cannot diagnose, check yourself out with a

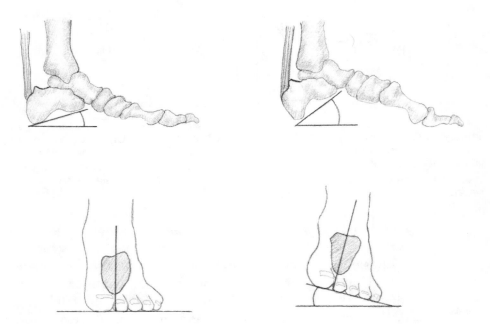

Abnormal foot structures can cause problems. In the normal arch (top left) the heel bone is at the proper angle. In the "cavus" (high-arched) foot (top right), the greater-than-normal pitch of the heel bone causes irritated tissues. A line drawn through the heel bone in a normal foot plant (bottom left) is perpendicular to the ground. With a forefoot varus condition, the heel bone is normal, but the forefoot tilts outward, causing a roll of the foot as it compensates.

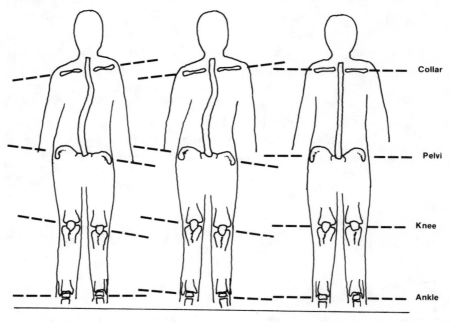

Collar

Pelvi

Knee

Ankle

This illustration gives you a view of what problems structure can cause and also shows that the problems can be brought under control. The first figure is of a person with one leg shorter than the other. It gets worse upon use (second figure) and can be corrected with orthotic inserts to restore balance (third figure).

podiatrist or sports-medicine specialist. It is a good idea to do this before you start jogging. Correcting any structural causes of injury early could save you a lot of problems later.

If you ignore these problems and continue to train despite the pain, you are not only foolish but risking the ability to run without pain. The pain will increase and force you to favor the injured area. This, in turn, will put excess pressure on another part of your body and possibly cause another injury.

If you get to the stage where you cannot run without favoring the injury, you should look for an alternative form of exercise to keep fit while the injury heals. Try biking, swimming, or walking if it does not aggravate the injury. Be sure to put ice or very cold water on the area for at least 48 hours after the injury. This will decrease the swelling and help to repair the damage. Once the scar tissue has been formed on the muscle tear and the bond gets stronger, you can apply heat to the area to improve circulation and help the body burn off excess fluid and waste. The injury is likely to be tender for quite a while after it heals.

What happens is, the muscle has been torn and bleeds, causing inflammation and pain. Scar tissue is formed to join the torn muscle fiber. The muscle begins to get stronger as the fibers reconnect and the scar tissue is gradually absorbed or shed by the muscle. The muscle is now healed and strong enough to handle full pressure again.

Once you have the full range of motion and the limb can bear the full weight or stress it used to, the damage is completely healed. In cold, damp weather, however, you are still likely to get minor soreness and stiffness in that area for as much as a year afterward.

If you are one of those who can't stop even though your body is trying very hard to tell you that you are doing something wrong, you will completely immobilize yourself. Your injury will become so severe you won't be able to walk without favoring the injured limb. You've reached the "pits." Running is out of the question, and even walking isn't doing you any good. At this stage, rest is the only thing that will heal the damaged muscle. You've ignored the warning, and so now you must pay the price. You've ignored prevention, and now you must take the cure, rest.

How do you prevent injuries? The best way is to heed the warnings when they come and back off until you are well. Take care in each of your runs to warm up before you go into any hard running. Use the first portion of your run to limber up and get into a rhythm. You can tell when you are stiff, tired, or sore. When these signs appear, make the run an easy one. You can always run hard tomorrow unless you ignore the warning and injure yourself first.

If you have to run on injuries, take steps to prevent them from getting any worse. Tape is one method. It is a flexible cast that keeps areas immobile. Since it can also put a strain on other muscles if it isn't done the right way, don't use it unless you know what you are doing.

Arch supports can clear up many problems in your feet and legs. Dr Scholl's arch supports or rubber arch cookies can be inserted in your shoes to help prevent problems. Plastic orthotics are the next step if you do not get relief from the arch supports. A podiatrist should be consulted if you have any problems you can trace to your feet.

If you have sore calves, try felt pads in your shoes to lift the heels slightly. Watch so this doesn't cause your feet to slip or slide in the shoes. A one-fourth to one-eighth-inch lift can help relieve some of the tension on your stretched calf muscles or Achilles tendons.

Pads can also be inserted toward the side of the shoe to correct an incorrect foot plant. This type of correction should be made by a podiatrist. Knee problems are usually a sign of improper foot strike and resulting pronation (inward rotation) of the leg. A good podiatrist will be able to diagnose and cure your problem.

I say a "good podiatrist" because not all are familiar with athletic injuries. Most doctors are taught how to cure problems rather than how to prevent them. Many doctors who come in contact with athletic injuries tell you "Don't run on it," which in many cases is not necessary. As was mentioned in the first part of this chapter, the injury comes in stages. For most injuries you can still maintain some activity and do not need to be immobile.

Immobility can be worse for the injury. The muscle will atrophy (shrink), and you will be forced to undertake a painful rehabilitation process to strengthen the muscle before

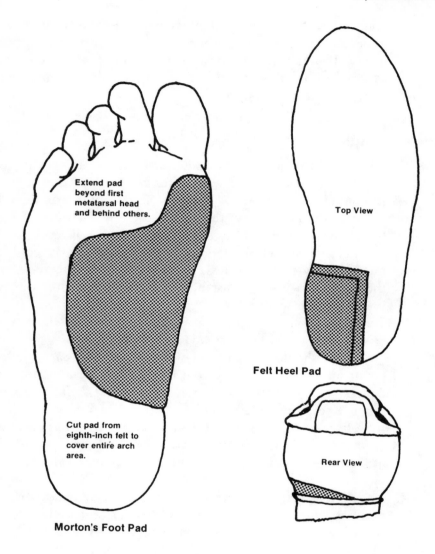

Extend pad beyond first metatarsal head and behind others.

Cut pad from eighth-inch felt to cover entire arch area.

Morton's Foot Pad

Top View

Felt Heel Pad

Rear View

This illustrates the use of an arch pad to remedy Morton's foot, a common problem caused by a person's second toe being longer than the first because of a short first metatarsal. Many people who have suffered stress fractures have this condition. If you have it, see a podiatrist. Also shown is the placement of a felt heel pad.

you can return to normal movement. This is why it is so important to slow down when you see the first signs of injury. If you don't and push it to the point where you have to stop completely, you face a long rehabilitation process after the damage is healed.

Handling colds

A cold is not quite as debilitating as an injury. It, too, has warning signs and in most cases can be limited in severity if you diagnose it soon enough. Some colds are like the "direct trauma" injury; they are caused by a virus that your body cannot fight off. It doesn't have any resistance to the disease, and the white blood cells can only make the cold less miserable by making it less severe. If you learn to recognize the signs of a lower resistance, you can prevent the diseases your body has already built a partial immunity against. If you don't get enough sleep or run your resistance down, you are risking being told by your body to slow down.

How should you treat a cold? For the most part, you can count on a week of sore throat followed by a runny nose and cough. The best place for you is in bed. Don't try to run when a cold hits unless it is very mild; then a very, very easy jog of about half your normal distance can help to "clean out your system." Your body is used to exercise, and this moderate effort maintains your routine without strain to your system.

You will feel the severity of the cold. When you run, if you can, you may be very weak. It may be an effort to jog for even a short distance. Minimize your effort. If it is too taxing, walk back home, take a shower, and go to bed.

Many pills and medications give you only symptomatic relief. For the common cold they won't help you get well any sooner, but they might relieve the symptoms enough that you don't feel so uncomfortable. If you can, let your body's defenses take care of the cold and forget the pills. Drugs can only substitute for natural substances that the body will have to produce to overcome the virus. The more you can rely on your own production of antibodies, the better. Many doctors admit this and tell you that the cold will last for seven days without the pills and a week with them. In other words, if you don't have to take them, don't. In cases of more severe illness (for example, flu or pneumonia), however, your body may need help to fight off the infection.

Drink a lot of fluids during this period, especially orange juice or liquids high in vitamin C. Don't eat heavy meals, but don't starve yourself. Eat foods that will be digested quickly and readily absorbed by the system. You will not be very hungry. One of the signs that your body is beginning to recover is renewed appetite. You should begin to feel better physically, and your runs can now be picked up a little.

Don't go right back to the level you were at before the cold. Take a week to work back up to the daily level you could do before, longer if you start to feel tired again.

A ten-percent hike in training mileage is said to be within limits. If you go over that amount, you are risking injury or colds. Take it easy. It will make your running healthier and happier.

Photo by Anne Kelly

5

Shoes

What is the right equipment for a jogger? What are the essentials, things you can't do without? A healthy body and two healthy legs for most people, and some manage without that much.

Jogging requires no exotic clothing. You can run naked on the beach, if you happen to own your own waterside retreat, or in a tuxedo. Your skin and your pocketbook will be the only things to suffer from either attire.

Seriously, you can jog in almost anything and your body will adapt to it eventually. The adaptation can be painful, however, and if you have any structural abnormalities in your feet or legs, you do need some form of extra support. Abnormally high arches or flat feet can cause problems, but they are not the subject of this chapter. For more information on them, see Chapter 4.

For now, we will concentrate on shoes. The first place to look when you want to buy equipment for jogging is the feet. Shoes are the most important item a jogger will purchase.

Selecting the right shoes

What is the difference between running shoes and other shoes? If I don't need any equipment to jog, why should I buy special shoes? Running shoes are designed to ease the stress on your feet and legs. Your dress or casual shoes are made to look good. Most of us do not walk around barefoot, which utilizes and stretches our foot and leg muscles. Most of us do not have perfectly balanced legs and feet.

The main villain is the elevated heel of our casual and dress shoes. This elevation inhibits the movement of the Achilles tendon and calf muscles. The muscles are never allowed to stretch fully during each stride, and as a result, they atrophy (shrink) because of lack of use. You will notice this if you change from regular footwear to the so-called negative heel shoes. Your calf muscles will be stiff and sore during the adjustment from one shoe to the other. The stiffness is caused by stretching the muscles you have not been utilizing to their full capacity. This is one of the reasons why a good heel is important in a running shoe, not because it is a necessary part of a good shoe but because it will ease the adjustment from walking to running by not forcing you to make the added change from an elevated heel to no elevation.

Most spiked shoes used by racers or those who trained on a track had no heel lift. This lead to very sore calf muscles after races and training sessions. Some spikes now have a minimal heel lift to prevent injuries to the legs of people who are using spikes for the first time.

Take a look at the wear pattern on the bottoms of your regular shoes. They will tell you how you land on your feet. This will give you an indication of what adjustments you may have to make in your shoes.

Before we delve into the world of pronation (a term meaning to turn downward with the inner surface of the foot) or supination (a term meaning to turn upward with the palm of the hand and forearm but used by podiatrists to mean when the heel bone tilts in and the leg externally rotates), I'll

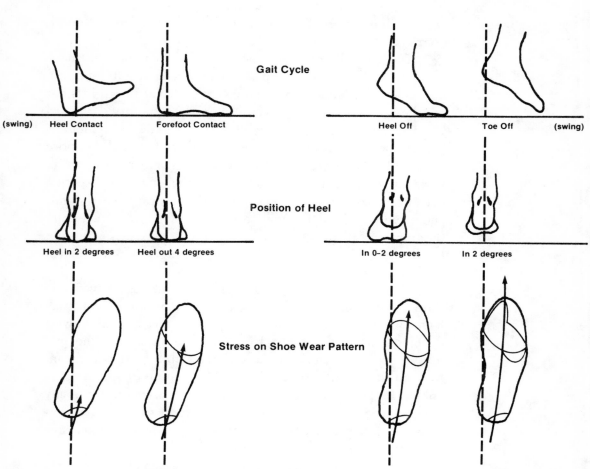

Gait Cycle

(swing) Heel Contact   Forefoot Contact

Heel Off   Toe Off   (swing)

Position of Heel

Heel in 2 degrees   Heel out 4 degrees

In 0-2 degrees   In 2 degrees

Stress on Shoe Wear Pattern

This shows you the normal wear pattern and foot placement during a normal stride.

attempt to describe in layman's terms how the feet and the legs operate during the gait cycle.

Your feet act first as shock absorbers and "mobile adaptors" from heel contact until your weight is shifted onto the ball of the foot. The foot then becomes a "rigid lever" in the propulsion mechanism of feet and legs acting together to push you forward. During this switch with your feet, your lower leg is rotating internally (counterclockwise) at heel contact and externally (clockwise) when you push off with your toes.

Try the following activity as you sit reading this chapter. Put your foot down on the heel as you would land in a normal stride. Now let your foot rock forward until it is flat on the ground. Look at your knee. It is pointing inward because your leg has rotated internally. The movement is hard to notice, but once you get up and walk, it will be more noticeable. Next, roll up onto your toes and push upward. Look at your knee. It is pointing in the opposite direction because it has rotated externally. The rotation is very slight, and it will be hard for you to notice unless you exaggerate the motion. If this motion is exaggerated when you run, however, you are pronating and supinating too much, and it could be a source of knee or leg problems.

What does all this physiological terminology have to do with shoes? Shoes can help you correct problems you may have with excessive rotation on your legs. The newest development is the flared heel for running shoes. The primary purpose of this innovation was stability. It was meant to keep those with weak ankles from twisting or spraining an ankle. As podiatrists began to find the causes for the many knee injuries they encountered, they soon suggested an expansion of the flared heel to help the person with excessive rotation because of improper foot plant.

Look at your wear pattern. You won't be able to examine your foot in motion to determine the exact angles that are indicated in the diagrams. If you have a normal wear pattern, don't worry about flared heels. If the wear on your shoes is unusual, for example, a lot of wear on the outside of the foot, see a podiatrist or get some extra-wide flared heels.

To correct your problem, a podiatrist may recommend arch supports instead of flared heels. This would be the case if your feet land too far toward the inside or arch of the foot. Arch supports will stabilize the feet and prevent that inward rotation. You may even need a plastic form of arch support

Gradual

Wide

A typical flared heel is wide at the base and gives you more stability. Flared heels range from gradual to radical. Most people can do well with the gradual flared heel.

known as an orthotic. How severe your problem is and what treatment to use should be left to the podiatrist. In many cases, a Dr. Scholl's arch support like the Flexo 610 or Athletic A will help, or the flared heel will solve your problem.

That's a long-winded way of giving you some information on heels. To put it in more concise terms, look for a stable heel (usually comes in the form of a solid heel cup) and a firm-layered, elevated heel. The layer nearest the sole should be soft to absorb shock and the other layer stiff to

An orthotic is made from a reverse cast of your foot. The right amount of compensation is then added to balance your feet and legs. Shown here is a side view of a plastic orthotic with a rearfoot post.

prevent the foot from rocking from side to side on a "mushy" heel.

A well-made shoe has these qualities plus a wide toe box, good support under the shank, or arch area, of the shoe, a built-in arch support, a flexible sole, and a comfortable fit. Nylon or nylon mesh with leather support pieces around the toe and heel areas is the best material for the upper of the shoe. It washes well and doesn't get stiff after getting wet. You may want to treat the leather areas with mink oil or some other solution to keep them flexible and somewhat water resistant. Leather gets stiff after a good soaking and will crack and cause blisters on your feet.

Blisters

Blisters are the direct result of friction. They can also be caused by a poor insole. Terry-cloth insoles have the same properties as leather after they get wet. They stiffen and bunch up, forming bumps and ridges that cause friction. The friction generates heat, which is transmitted to the skin. To protect itself from overheating, the skin sweats. If this doesn't cool off the area, the outer layer of skin separates from the inner layer and a pocket of fluid serves as insulation in between. If the inner layer is still being rubbed, it bleeds and forms a blood blister.

To prevent blisters, keep your shoes from getting stiff or worn so that ridges or lumpy surfaces won't form. If you do get a blister, repair the shoe or get a new pair. If you have enough toe room in the shoe (it is recommended that you have one finger's width of room between your toes and the end of the shoe) and a good insole (Spenco—a type of rubber impregnated by nitrogen covered with a layer of woven silk fiber), you will minimize your blisters.

Always wear socks. It will prevent your shoes from becoming "ripe" from your sweat and reduce blisters. Socks made of a combination of Orlon, nylon, and cotton seem to hold up the best after repeated washings. All-cotton socks tend to deteriorate and become rough after washing. The combination of materials keeps fluffy for a longer period of time and doesn't irritate your feet.

A flexible sole can also prevent blister problems. If the sole is too stiff, it will not bend with your feet as you lift with your toes to push off. This will cause the heel area to slide down some and cause friction and pressure on the Achilles tendon. It also makes the foot work harder because of the resistance of the shoe.

Blisters can cause harmful side effects if they are not treated properly. You will begin favoring the limb with the blister and putting more pressure on the other leg. This could cause an overuse injury on that particular foot or leg.

The proper treatment of a blister involves taking the pressure off the blistered area. Cut a piece of moleskin or felt padding so that it forms a circle around the blister and does not touch the tender area. If you have a blister on your big toe, you might consider cutting a hole in the toe area of an old pair of shoes to reduce contact with the blistered area. Vaseline should be spread over the blister to prevent friction.

The shoe bends right at the metatarsal joint. A good flexible shoe will be able to do this without great strain.

You should soak the foot in soapy water or in Epsom salts to dry out the blister under the layer of dead tissue. The fluid should be drained from the blister, with care taken not to infect the area. The dead skin should be removed as soon as it becomes stiff or the skin underneath is no longer sensitive to the touch.

No shoe made today has a really good arch support. As long as they are not cut away under the arch, or shank area, and have a rubber arch cookie, they will be acceptable. If you do need extra support in this area, try the arch supports mentioned earlier in this chapter. If you can, glue them into the shoe once you find the correct placing. Put a Spenco insole over them to reduce friction and glue it down. This will necessitate trying on your shoes with the support and Spenco to get a correct fit.

When fitting yourself for shoes, look for comfort. Always stand up and walk around in them. Measure your toe room while standing up, not while you are sitting down. The feet expand as you stand up, and they also expand as you run. In warm weather your feet will seem larger, also. Try both shoes on when you are getting a fitting; sometimes one foot is larger or smaller than the other.

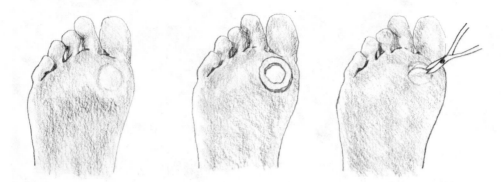

First isolate the blister and put a pad around it. When it has healed and the skin has dried, remove the dead skin.

Caring for your shoes

Take care to repair your shoes properly. There are many products on the market today that will add life to your shoes. Glue guns, shoe goo, and the like will add miles to the shoe without taking dollars from your pocket. Don't hang on to an old pair too long, however, or you are risking injury. Once the upper starts to shred or the heel counter (heel cup) begins to break down, it is time for a new pair. You can replace the insole and goo the worn spots on your heel, but you can't repair an unstable heel.

One more tip, when the nubs on your waffle-soled shoes begin to wear, you can't goo each nub separately. Before they get worn more than halfway down, put a layer of goo along the area covering several nubs. This will increase the effectiveness of the repair. Be sure to keep the level of the goo even with the healthy nubs. Take care of your shoes and they will do their job; let them get too worn and you're inviting injury.

If you have proper shoes, you have the right equipment. The rest of your wardrobe is merely for comfort, style, or defense against the weather.

Photo by Anne Kelly

6

Clothing

After you've chosen your shoes, you can move on to the other parts of your wardrobe. This is where you can really have fun. None of it is necessary except to help you handle different weather conditions.

There is no "in" look in jogging, though marketing executives across the country are trying to create one. If there is a national uniform of the jogger, it is possibly the T-shirt. Here is your chance to be a trend setter in fashion, while maintaining a practical wardrobe for all weather.

Warm weather garb

First, we'll cover summer fashion, then move on to your fall and winter wardrobe. The spring and the summer are really the critical times. You'll have the most trouble if you dress wrong during this portion of the year, and what you choose forms the basic set for your whole outfit. Look for something light and durable. These items will be washed and abused more than any other clothing you own. Look for quality and good craftsmanship.

Your shorts should be made of nylon. Cotton stiffens and chafes after a few washings. Many shorts include briefs. This cuts your wear and tear on underwear and is an added convenience. Some shorts are made out of the same material as swim trunks and dry quickly and without stiffness. A pair can be dried during the night and be ready for wear the next morning. While this is convenient during a trip, you should always alternate pairs. The same with your shoes. Have two pairs so that one can air out and sit for a day. This will add to the life of your shoes and clothing. Repeated wear adds to the deterioration of the article.

T-shirts, as I mentioned, are the rage with the jogging crowd. They bear the names of shoe manufacturers, races, cities, and everything else imaginable. The one thing to be careful of with a T-shirt is the lettering or design on it. If it is silk-screened and heavily inked, it may rub on your nipples. Many marathoners experience this with a normal shirt, but these heavy designs are stiff and will rub you raw over a shorter distance. If you have this problem with your T-shirts, I would recommend that you tape your nipples to prevent rubbing, as do many marathoners. Most joggers do not have this trouble because it normally takes a long distance for the rubbing to be that severe.

For women, running with or without a bra is dependent upon personal preference. Big-breasted women would probably be more comfortable with a bra. There is no known muscle damage from the bouncing of the breasts during jogging, but a bra would decrease the movement. At this time, there are no bras on the market made specifically for women joggers. A smooth, regular support bra is recommended. It should be tight fitting but not confining. Women should also be aware of the chafing of the nipples and take precautions along with the men. Women are particularly sensitive in this area during menstruation.

Mesh shirts are best in summer for men, with bikini tops preferred by women. The mesh lets the heat out and the air in to cool the body. Wear as little as possible on hot, humid days. The humidity doesn't allow the heat to escape as readily because your sweat does not evaporate quickly.

You'll feel the heat first in your head. It will feel like you could fry an egg up there. Pour water over your head and take along a plant-spray bottle to cool yourself. The spray works better than dumping water on yourself because it covers a greater area and doesn't end up in your socks and shoes to make your feet feel like anchors.

If you start to get dizzy or disoriented, STOP RUNNING! Find some shade and something to cool off with. If you've stopped sweating, it is another sign your body has overheated. Get out of the sun, get cool, and relax. You're risking possible brain damage from heatstroke if you try to push yourself. Don't fool around in hot weather. It can lead only to trouble.

During the summer or on hot days, run in the early morning or in the cool of the evening. You are not training to acclimate your body to the heat as the racer does who has to race under those conditions. Stay away from the hot portions of the day. Nobody feels good running in the heat.

Cold weather dressing

The other extreme is not quite so dangerous. You can run on the coldest days of winter if you take precautions to dress right and stay away from heavy winds, which can cause the windchill to be far below zero even on moderately cold days. You can always put more clothes on for a cold day than you can take off for a terribly hot day. The best way to beat the cold is to dress in layers. You have your basic outfit from the summer. Shorts, socks, and shirt form the undergarments, with a cotton sweat suit added for the mild winter days. The sweat-suit top should have a hood with a string for closing the neck portion. A good shirt for the winter is an old turtleneck. It keeps the cold wind off your neck and gives you an extra layer of protection. If you need another layer under your sweat pants, try long johns. Many people dye them and use them as sweat bottoms with the shorts worn on the outside.

Whatever makes up the outer layer, make sure it closes off the wind. The wrists, the ankles, the neck, and the waist are areas where a draft can get in under the outer layer. Keep these areas tight so that the cold air won't get inside. Also, if you sweat too much or get parts of your clothes wet, they lose their insulation properties. This is why it is good practice to run against the wind the first part of your run and with the wind the second half. Coming home against a cold wind can give you a chill.

The best protection in the winter is a nylon rain suit over your sweats. This keeps in the heat and keeps out the cold wind. Make sure it is flexible nylon, not plastic. Plastic cracks when it is cold, but nylon remains pliable.

Always wear a hat during the winter, preferably a stocking cap that will cover your ears. Since most of the body's heat is lost through the head, keep it covered in the winter. On very cold days you may want to wear a ski mask with eyeholes. A surgeon's mask is also useful if your lungs have trouble with cold weather.

To protect your hands, wear mittens, which are better than gloves because they pool the heat of the entire hand rather than isolate single fingers. Your fingers and feet are the first things to notice the cold on most days; so protect your hands and keep your feet moving. No special care is needed for the feet except to keep them from getting wet.

Keep your ankles covered. Don't leave them exposed, with only one thin layer of sock protecting them against the wind. They will get chapped and the skin will break. Keep your sweat pants down as far as you can and wear a thin sock underneath your outer sock if you have to, but keep the wind off your ankles.

Many companies make special nylon rain suits like this one. If you don't want to spend the money, at least buy a nylon windbreaker for the winter months.

Coping with special conditions

For those of you who live in areas afflicted by white rain, otherwise known as snow, there are certain adjustments you have to make. The first is to find a route that is relatively free from traffic. When snow turns to ice, the roads get slick and a car that could normally stop may not. Most winter running has to be done in the streets unless your neighbors shovel their sidewalks. Always run against traffic so that you can see what's coming and have more chances to avoid any problems.

Slippery streets are a sure way to teach you to shorten your stride. Long striders, many times, end up with sore posteriors because their stride is not compatible with the forces of nature. When you overstride, your center of gravity is not directly over your feet when your heel makes contact with the ground. When the heel begins to slip on the ice, you are not in balance enough to prevent a long slide and possibly a fall.

If you would like a good resistance workout, try running through the unplowed snow. This forces you to lift your knees high and soon adds some weight to your feet from the snow accumulated on them. This can be a very tough workout. Just make sure the snow is not hiding holes in the ground where you could twist an ankle or worse.

For any time of the year, especially winter, it is always better to overdress than underdress. You can always take something off, but if you don't have it, you can't put something on to battle the cold.

On a fashion note, stay away from the flared bottoms on the pants of track suits. They are nice for a dressy look or for tennis players, but for runners they let in air on the legs and get in the way. Stay with the regular-cut legs and try to get a pair that is loose fitting. Skintight pants are more restricting.

Your aim is not to look good but to stay warm in the winter and cool in the summer. Choose your clothes. with these goals in mind and if you can mix fashion and comfort, more power to you. You can be the Bill Blass or Yves Saint-Laurent of running fashion.

Photo by Bernie Friel

7
Diet

Weight control and jogging are linked in the minds of many people so, obviously, we need a chapter on diet, not just for those who are watching their weight but for anyone who mixes running and eating. The big question is, how do you mix running and eating? Running and eating don't mix. One sustains the other, but when you mix them both together, you encounter some unpleasant complications.

When and how much to eat

Digestion stops when running begins. Your body can't digest food and metabolize it at the same time. It is best to wait at least three hours after a meal before you exercise. Side aches, cramps, and an upset stomach are some of the results of eating too close to exercise. Your eating and exercise habits should be in harmony, not at war. You have to mix the two components into your life-style, not force one in on top of the other.

Most people eat too much. This is a sweeping statement that is bound to get me into trouble. But the statistics back me up. A "normal" individual has about 10 to 14 percent of his body weight in fat. (This is for males; the female is slightly higher, about 16 percent.) An obese individual has 20 percent (30 percent for females), while world-class distance runners have below 6 percent.

Distance runners need energy and calories to perform. Yet an average distance runner will eat quite a bit less, comparatively, than a normal individual. Their calorie level is usually higher, but so is their energy expenditure. Most runners snack during the major portion of the day and eat a good meal in the evening after their running for the day is done. A three-full-meals-a-day runner is rare. For every 3,500 kilocalories you consume, one pound of fat is added to your system. Runners burn up a lot of calories and add only a little.

This is the key to balancing your weight. You can't run and expect to eat more and still lose weight. You have to eat the same amount or less before you will lose weight. Exercise gives you no excuse to overindulge. To lose weight, you have to burn up the available calories in the system and then your body converts to utilizing your body fat for energy. Weight loss occurs as you use up more fat than you replace.

Very hard exercise in women can lead to a lowered fat level and loss of menstruation. Doctors do not know whether a hormonal imbalance or the lowered fat level directly cause the loss of menstruation. The condition clears up once the woman stops intense training; so there seems to be no danger of sterility, just a temporary and unreliable form of birth control. (See Chapter 9.)

The great majority of runners don't train at that level. A good indicator of the severity of your workouts is the smell of the clothes after a run. In a hard run you lose more of the minerals and fluids in your system, and your clothes are particularly "ripe" afterward, while after an easy run the smell is milder.

What to eat

I'm not going to attempt to give you a sample diet to

follow. Everyone is so different, with different tastes and different needs, that it would be useless. Most foods in moderation are good for you. Some have qualities that make them more attractive to the runner than others. Chicken, seafood, and turkey are easier to digest than some of the fatty meats like beef or pork. Proteins in general take longer to digest than fats or carbohydrates. It will usually take a couple of hours for proteins to be broken down by your system. Fats take a little less time, while carbohydrates are the quick energy foods. Coffee, tea, or cola are good diuretics because of the caffeine they contain. Breads, as well as all starchy, doughy foods, tend to sit in your stomach.

This is a fact you know well if you've ever had to make a "pit stop" during your run. Many runners have started to carry toilet paper with them after running too close to a meal.

You should be able to tell when you are carrying too much. Everyone is familiar with the bloated feeling after not being able to turn down mom's apple pie or some other taste treat that we really didn't need. Learn to refuse gracefully or ask for a doggie bag at restaurants.

It is also best to wait for at least a half hour after your run before you sit down to eat. An hour is even better. Give your body a chance to wind down from the run. You can sip on some liquid refreshments to quench your thirst or have a small appetizer, but your system is generally not ready for a heavy meal after a run.

Just as you will know when to stop, you won't need to be told when you are ready to eat. Eat your food slowly; don't attack the food, savor it. The right foods will satiate your appetite and refresh you. Too much food will make you drowsy and bloated. You don't need more calories to sustain your jogging. Jogging isn't for those who want an excuse to eat more food. In fact, in a moderate jogging program, most people experience a decrease in appetite, not an increase. They run instead of eat during their lunch break. It helps them lose weight and exercise at the same time.

Try saving your favorite meals or a trip to your favorite restaurant until the evening after a hard workout or race.

You can relax after the hard work and savor the mental high of a job well done along with the reward of your favorite meal.

Supplements

This brings us to vitamins. Most people don't need them. Many people take them out of habit or because their friends do. At the beginning of an exercise program they may help you adjust to the increase in activity, but once you are reasonably fit, you may no longer need the extra vitamins. Former Olympian and ABC Sports commentator Marty Liquori once said about vitamin-pill poppers, "All they have is expensive urine." Most vitamins do little harm because they are eliminated from your system. Therefore, if you feel you need them, they can't hurt you when taken in moderation. The evidence for vitamin C is mixed. Some people indicate that it helps prevent colds and repair damaged muscle tissue. None of this has ever been proved, but if it makes you feel more secure, take it.

In regard to fluid replacement during your run, water is still the best. Special drinks like ERG (electrolyte replacement with glucose) are mostly potassium based and could possibly cause cramps if you drink too much. Most of it just flows right out of your system. Your body does not absorb much during exercise, and you would be forced to drink much more than you could stand of the replacement fluids to benefit significantly from them. So drink water, preferably cold, because cold liquids are absorbed into your system faster. After the run is the time for the ERG. Don't consume large amounts right away. Drink it slowly and give it a chance to get into your system. You'll start urinating when your body has enough of that particular fluid. You'll feel like drinking a lake, but resist the urge and take it in doses.

The same with dieting and running. Don't attempt to lose too much at once. Any great shift in weight or loss of anything has a marked effect on the body. The body adjusts best when it can do it gradually. This is trying on the patience of many people, but it is kindest to the system.

Jogging and eating are lifetime activities. Blend them into your system and they will work in harmony to bring you a better quality of life. You will have more energy and be able to enjoy fully the simple pleasures of life, like a good meal.

Photo by Anne Kelly

8

Preparing for competition

Not long ago a fellow named Dr. Delano Meriwether was watching a track meet on television with his wife. His attention was focused on the sprinting events.

"I could run as fast as those guys," Meriwether said. His wife challenged him to prove it.

About a year and a half after he began training, 27-year-old hematologist Del Meriwether tied the world record for the 100-yard dash and won the national championship. An overnight success story—well, not quite.

While many of you may share the same aspirations, you better be aware of what you're in for before you make your reservations for Moscow in 1980. There are many levels of competition, and if you are intelligent in your approach to training and possess some talent, you can be successful in some form at your level.

Meriwether did not start training just on a whim. He was not an out-of-shape old man trying to stop the advance of old age. He had kept himself fit, and the only reason he had never competed was that the demands of medical school were too much to include a track career.

When he did begin his training, he had an international-level 400-meter Olympic hurdler to train with, and he worked out only sparingly at first. He suffered pulled muscles and similar setbacks, but his talent and dedication were enough to overcome these obstacles.

If you've never run a step in your life, chances are you are not quite ready for competition at this level. There are a variety of alternatives available, from jogger's races to Masters competition for those over 40 years of age. The Amateur Athletic Union (AAU) has age-group running programs for kids that start with a nine-and-under group and go in groups of two (10-11, 12-13, etc.) up through the teenage years. Competition is open to everyone regardless of age or ability. There is even a category for those between 30 and 40 years old called sub-Masters.

So if you've always had the urge to race, there is a forum for you somewhere. Most cities have running clubs or organizations that promote the sport. They usually have race schedules and know whom to contact for races. There are national organizations, like the Road Runners Club of America and the National Jogging Association (NJA) that can also provide you with the needed information. For information about the Road Runners Club, contact Jeff Darman, 2737 Devonshire Place NW, Washington, D.C. 20008. The NJA contact is Rory Donaldson, 1910 K Street NW #202, Washington, D.C. 20006.

Training

A lot of people judge success in running by the time they are able to achieve. It gives them a clear goal toward which to direct their training. Others like the spirit of competition, pitting oneself against another in a test of will and stamina. It is also a test of your training. I say training, not just running or jogging, because to race well, you have to train.

Training involves planning your goal and using certain forms of running to prepare your body to achieve that goal. Training is specific exercise that prepares you for the varying stresses of a race. Your daily run is usually at one speed, with little variation. Most races involve a variety of speeds, depending on the level of competition.

These changes in speed require tactics and produce more stress, both mental and physical. It is important to approach a race with a clear impression of what you are capable of doing and what you would like to achieve. If your fastest quarter mile is 75 seconds, you shouldn't be planning on running a five-minute mile. Through your training, you should get an idea of what you are capable of running and plan your race accordingly. If you go into a race without any idea of what your maximum speed is or how fit you are, you run the risk of trying to go too fast and building up a huge oxygen debt early in the race. This inhibits your movement, makes you less efficient, and, worst of all, hurts.

In your training you should attempt to divide your entire race into portions. Run those parts for time to determine what speed you can handle comfortably and establish your goal for the entire race accordingly. This type of training is called interval training. It is usually done on the track or in some area where you have measured the specific distance you want to run. For example, if you were racing a mile, you would run a set of four quarter miles with a quarter-mile walk or jog between each interval. You run the quarters hard but not at full effort. If you can run each of them easily in 90 seconds, a good goal for you may be a six-minute mile. You would not be able to run this right away unless it was extremely easy to run each of the four quarter miles in 90 seconds; then you would readjust your goals.

This is putting the cart before the horse, however, because before you start any interval training, you have to have a good distance base to work from. This means that you should have done a lot of longer, even-paced runs to build up your aerobic capacity. This is your basic endurance work. Aerobic capacity is your ability to utilize oxygen in the chemical reaction that powers muscle contraction. In walking you are functioning aerobically because your system is taking in enough oxygen to operate the muscles.

When you shift into a run, you build an oxygen deficit. The rapid shift in energy needs leaves the system without enough available oxygen to carry on the chemical reaction entirely with oxygen. Lactic acid is substituted in the process. As you begin to breathe deeper and your system reaches a point known as the steady state, this deficit is paid back and you are operating aerobically again. The steady state is generally the upper level of your system's ability to operate aerobically. If you increase your speed from the steady state, you are running into oxygen debt. The debt must be paid off by slower running or walking to allow the system to regain sufficient oxygen to once again operate aerobically.

Jogging and distance running increase your aerobic capacity by strengthening the heart muscle to allow it to pump more blood into the system with each stroke or beat. Jogging also increases the number of capillaries in the muscle tissue, which in turn helps the blood transport more oxygen into the tissue so that it can operate aerobically at a higher rate of contraction or higher speed.

This is the primary benefit of jogging, and if you do nothing but distance training, you will improve just by getting stronger and more aerobically fit. Runs of 30 minutes a day four times a week are enough to maintain a minimum level of good fitness. This training increases your endurance by making the body more efficient. It improves the transport system for blood and oxygen in your system and enables you to operate at higher speeds aerobically and pay off oxygen debt quickly. When you reach the point where you can do at least an average of 30 minutes of running a day, every day, you have a good distance base. This base is essential for performing the more taxing, varied speed training necessary for racing.

During your distance runs you should be running comfortably. When you switch to faster speeds in the training runs, you will be extending yourself past the comfort zone. In racing you seldom operate in the comfort zone; your opponent tries to make you hurt to get you to slow down or quit. This is where the test of will comes into running. You are the one who determines when to hold back or when it hurts too much. The casual racer backs off at the first sign of pain, but the top competitors push until the opposition lets go or there is nothing left to push with.

Your muscles operate on lactic acid instead of oxygen and they slow down in their contractions. You get slower and feel heavy. Soon the level of discomfort and lactic acid buildup is too much and you stop. Every runner has his own level of discomfort. He finds it in training and racing and backs off when he reaches that level. If other runners are fitter or better that day, the prize is theirs. You go back and work on having a better day, or maybe you reached your goal even though you didn't win the race.

Goals

Racing is mainly to define your limits, not those of others. If you go into racing just to beat another, your racing career will be dictated by others rather than yourself. Your risk of injury is higher because you forget your own limitations for the moment and try to push too hard to reach someone else's level. You should train to maximize your performance and be content to do your best. If someone else is better on a particular day, look for the reasons why and plan to improve in the future.

You can't control another person's performance. You can play tricks on him with a variety of tactics, like starting out fast or running portions of the race at varying paces to throw off his rhythm. You are working with the mind of the other person in these cases, and that is an unpredicatable element. Physical capacity and performance are sometimes easily predictable, but the mental side of racing is not. This is what makes it so exciting. It is the test of one runner's will and wits against another's. The result can change from day to day.

Fartlek

But let's get back to the physical side once again because that is where you build confidence in your ability. After you've got a distance base, you'll want to try to vary your pace during your long runs. You can increase your strength by incorporating hill runs into your route and occasionally running what is known as *fartlek.*

Fartlek is a Swedish word meaning speed play. In a *fartlek* run you vary your speed according to the goal of the workout and how you feel. If you want to mix up the pace in your next race, you'll want to run fast for portions of your distance run, slow down, and then speed up again. This gives your body a chance to adapt to changing speeds and shifting from aerobic to anaerobic conditions. *Fartlek* is also a bridge between straight distance work and interval training. In essence, it is an unstructured form of interval training that can be done anywhere rather than on a track. *Fartlek* and hill training add to your strength and prepare your muscles for the added stress of interval training and racing.

Whatever system you are using, it is best to follow a hard/easy pattern. One day you may run a hard session of *fartlek,* hills, or intervals. The next day is a relaxed, easy run to let the system rest and store energy for the next hard session.

When you are training anaerobically, you upset the chemical balance of your system. This leads to tiredness, depression, and possible injury. If you do too much interval training, you upset the acid/base balance in your system. That is one reason intervals are not recommended until near the end of your season or the final phase before peaking for your most important race. In any case, they are to be used sparingly. Don't run intervals every other day on a hard/easy training pattern. You may not be able to go hard/easy at first, anyway. It may take you two days to recover from a hard workout or race before you can attempt another hard run. Take two or three days, if you need, to recover. A runner who is not quite sharp will do a better job in a race than one who is exhausted or injured.

Take your time

Training is a gradual process. It takes weeks, months, and years to build your system to the point where it is performing at its maximum. Frank Shorter did not become Olympic champion in 1972 from 1971's training alone. It took him years to build up to the peak he attained at Munich, and he is still building.

Continual hard running and racing will leave you mentally and physically stale. Plan your year or seasons with easy races, as well as those toward which you are pointing your training. Every race can be a great race if you maintain sensible goals. You will improve for a period of time and then level off. You then must build to a higher level to attain a higher peak. Your jogging, *fartlek,* hills, and intervals combine with your racing to reach a few peaks each year.

Each person is different, but there is a formula that is used by most of the top distance runners today. It involves averaging a certain number of miles a day during the full year. The exact distance varies according to the length of the race you are preparing for. You have periods of the year when you are running more miles to establish a better base for your faster training and some when you are running less to let the body recover and rest for races.

You can't train and race successfully at the same time, not during your peak season. You can incorporate races into your training pattern, but these races are really nothing more than fast training runs. They fit into the formula as speed workouts or hard distance runs.

Most successful distance runners have three days a week of hard work and the rest easy distance or run-as-you-feel distance work. A typical pattern would be a mix of different types of interval or *fartlek* runs on, say, Monday, Wednesday, and Friday. A race could substitute for one of the distance interval workouts. Then one day a week an extra long run is added. The fast work is done at or below race pace, the speed you would like to run the race at. The long distance run is between 15 and 30 miles, depending on your event. During their training marathoners like to run a distance close to the complete race to prepare them for the long grind of the marathon.

Stated physiologically training for racing is preparation for accepting anaerobic stress and performance at a higher level of aerobic fitness. You train at your racing speed for portions of your overall program to let the body and mind adapt to this stress. You run long to maintain a high level of aerobic fitness, which is the base of all your other training.

There are periods for "rest" in this schedule also. A training program runs in peaks and valleys. You build up to a peak and then relax the training to let the body rest. You start building again to another peak. Each time the peak gets higher as your condition improves.

This is the benefit of a year-long program. It may get you to your goals slowly, but it gets you there gradually and without a serious threat of injury. You have times when you are most vulnerable when you are training the hardest, and others when your resistance is high. You can run races for fun, with no investment of maximum effort, to judge your condition and how your training has progressed.

Your racing can be as enjoyable as the rest of your running. You just have to fit it into your life-style like your jogging program. This chapter is a mere outline of what you can do. You have to fill in the specifics. The principle is the same: mix stress with rest to improve your overall condition.

There is no joy like accomplishing a feat you didn't expect. Here you've been training for a long time trying to break a barrier, say, run a five-minute mile. You ran a 5:15 the week before in what seemed like an all-out effort. You are discouraged and get more rest than usual during the following week. A friend challenges you to run a mile with him on the weekend, and you accept, not expecting to do well because of your disappointment over the past week's effort. You come through the first quarter mile in 73 seconds feeling fine, the half comes in 2:25, and you are gaining confidence and strength. At three-quarters of a mile you are 3:40 and that five-minute mile is 440 yards away. You charge the last quarter in 70 seconds and total 4:50 for the mile, shattering your personal best. The feeling of accomplishment makes you forget any discomfort you may have felt during the run. You've done it! After all the work, the goal has been reached.

This is but one of the joys of being fit. You will discover many others in the months and years ahead. The only limitations are the time and effort you devote to your exercise. The fun has just begun.

Photo by Jim Ferstle

9
Questions and answers

Q: How do you make running a part of your life-style?

A: You have to make the commitment to include running in your everyday activity. You also have to be willing to give it a chance to take hold. One week or one month is not enough time to form a pattern of behavior.

Generally, three months of a consistent program will get you started. If you can maintain your routine for that long, you will have set a pattern that you are not likely to break. Once you've been running regularly for three months, you will be aware of the problems and the pleasures of the activity and will have a better understanding of your commitment to an exercise program.

Q: Should you breathe through your nose or through your mouth?

A: Both if you can. It is important to inhale as much oxygen as you can, and there is no one proper way to accomplish this. Whatever is natural for you will probably work best.

The important thing is to maintain proper posture to allow your body to breathe in and out without restrictions. If you are bent over or forward, you are restricting the movement of your diaphragm. This can keep you from getting all the oxygen you should from each breath. It is a common mistake made by tired runners after a race. They bend over from fatigue and thereby restrict their supply of oxygen. This hinders their recovery. It is better to stand straight or lay flat, if you have to, to let the air in and out easily.

Q: What causes side aches or side stitch, and how can I prevent them from bothering me when I run?

A: There are three theoretical causes of side aches. One is trapped oxygen in the bronchial tubes of the lungs. Another is too much blood in the abdominal region. The third is improper digestion of food.

To relieve the first cause, you do an exercise called belly breathing. Hold your hand on your diaphragm and breathe in and out. If you are like most people, you will notice that you do much of your breathing with your chest rather than with the diaphragm. Get down on all fours and breathe. Notice the breathing is controlled by the diaphragm rather than the chest. This is belly breathing, using your diaphragm. When air gets trapped in the lungs, breathe against resistance. Grunt or breathe out while holding your hand over the diaphragm as resistance. This should get rid of the trapped air.

If the cause of your problem is too much blood in the abdomen, you can correct this by reversing the blood flow. Stand on your head or do a shoulder stand to make the blood flow out of the region.

The final cause, improper digestion, is best avoided by not running too close to your meals. You can try massaging the area, but the only real solution is not to mix eating and running.

Q: What about resistance training or weight training?

A: Resistance training comes in many forms. Running on

hills, on soft sand, or against stiff winds. It is good for developing strength and has a part in the program of every distance runner.

For the jogger or noncompetitive runner it can be used to vary the conditions of the run, but its main function is to condition the competitive athlete. It is generally pretty demanding physically and can lead to injuries in the improperly conditioned runner.

Most runners run hills or on sand occasionally, and this helps to vary the effort in a run. Hill training involves repeated running up and down hills to increase the stamina of the runner. It is done between the long distance running phase of training and the interval or sharpening phase. It serves as a form of transition between the distance-based long runs and the shorter, faster interval workouts. It increases the stress and prepares the body for speed workouts.

Weights can be used if the runner feels the need for adding upper body strength. You shouldn't lift weights with your legs unless you intend to strengthen a muscle weak from injury. Weight lifting for distance runners should consist of many repetitions with light weights. This builds endurance strength rather than muscle bulk. You really don't need weights to improve your running. The actual running action itself puts enough stress on the muscles you use to adequately strengthen them for your activity. In the case of weak muscles or injuries, a rehabilitation program can be attempted with weights to rejuvenate injured limbs.

Q: Does wearing a rubber sweat suit help you lose weight while exercising?

A: Wearing a rubber sweat suit isn't the key to losing weight. You usually end up drinking or eating more calories after the run than you burned during the exercise. The secret to losing weight is simple. Energy output (exercise) must exceed energy input (food consumption).

A regular exercise program can help you beat your weight problem by improving muscle tone and lifting your metabolic rate, the rate at which your body uses up energy. When you exercise, the rate increases, and it maintains a higher level than normal for as much as six hours afterward. This burns off a lot of calories.

You may not notice the weight loss immediately because your gain in muscle weight may equal your loss in fat. You'll notice the difference in muscle tone by the way your clothes fit, however, and soon the weight will begin to drop also as long as you don't increase your food intake.

Q: Can I wear my running shoes all the time and for other sports?

A: No, running shoes were made for running. The nylon uppers of many brands will tear if used for stop-and-go sports like basketball or tennis. They were made to withstand the pressures of running, not other sports. You shouldn't wear them to walk around in because you will decrease their life span. It is best to have two pairs for running. Wear one on one day and give it a rest by using the second pair the following day. This gives the shoe material time to dry and air out. It will prolong the life of your shoes.

Q: What about running during pregnancy?

A: Most doctors agree that if you were running regularly before you became pregnant, you can keep running while pregnant. You shouldn't start running during pregnancy and should consult your doctor before continuing your running during pregnancy, even if you are already an active runner.

Women who have run during their pregnancy report easier deliveries and a faster recovery. Running relaxes them and gives them better muscle control. Mileage and effort naturally decrease as the time of delivery nears, but a running program can be maintained through most of the pregnancy.

Q: What about menstruation—does running help or hinder it?

A: Menstruation is a subject many doctors are just now

beginning to examine thoroughly. It has always suffered from the psychological stigma of being a disease or "curse" that the women had to bear. It is not: it is the natural cycle of the reproductive system.

Exercise has affected the cycle in ways that are just beginning to be studied. Amenorrhea, or absence of menstruation, is a condition that occurs in some women for a variety of reasons. Some are structural or hormonal and should be treated by a doctor. Secondary amenorrhea, or absence of regular menstruation after menstruation has already occurred, happens when a woman is pregnant or breast-feeding. It can also occur as a reaction to stress, fear, or emotional trauma. Some women experience secondary amenorrhea while training intensely. One woman reported not menstruating for four years while training heavily for racing. Her regular cycle returned when she relaxed from hard training.

This person also had a very low percentage of body fat and the question being studied now is whether the low level of body fat triggered a chemical change to stop the regular menstrual cycle or whether a hormonal change occurred because the heavy exercise lowered her fat level and/or changed the hormonal balance to disrupt the menstrual flow. It is an area of study of significance to all hard-training women athletes.

Dysmenorrhea is a problem that most women face in one form or another during menstruation. Dysmenorrhea is the catchword for menstrual or premenstrual pain and discomfort. It comes in two forms, spasmodic and congestive.

Spasmodic dysmenorrhea is marked by spasms of dull and/or acute pain in the lower abdomen. It is localized pain, usually involving only the lower abdomen and genital area. The current theory is that it is caused by a hormonal imbalance, too much progesterone in relation to estrogen.

Congestive dysmenorrhea occurs just before the onset of menstruation. It involves a dull aching in the lower abdomen;

bloatedness and swelling of the tissues in the abdomen, breasts, genitals, or extremities; headache and backache; nausea, constipation, and/or diarrhea; pains in the joints; and general feelings of depression, fatigue, tension, and irritability. These symptoms may or may not occur in everyone, only a few in some, more in others. Their cause is the opposite imbalance in hormones as that theorized to cause spasmodic dysmenorrhea, that is, too much estrogen in relation to progesterone.

Exercise helps in the care of spasmodic dysmenorrhea by improving the muscle tone and relaxing the muscles. Specific exercises for the pelvic region or heating pads are other recommended treatments. A relatively salt-free diet, along with mild diuretics, helps in controlling water retention. Watching your intake of fluids is also advised. Hormonal therapy is being experimented with for mood changes and prevention of some of the problems of dysmenorrhea, but much work is still to be done in this area.

Generally, exercise helps build your tolerance to discomfort and increases your resistance to fatigue. Both these factors can help minimize the physical discomfort of dysmenorrhea. The most positive effect of exercise is that it helps one relate better with one's body. It increases the amount of oxygen in the body, and research has shown that a problem-free menstrual period is closely tied to the proper amount of oxygen in the body and to the flow of oxygen-carrying blood to all the systems and organs. Regular exercise strengthens both your respiratory and circulatory systems and can help diminish menstrual problems.

Q: Is there an easy way to take your mind off discomfort while running, besides trying to look at the scenery? What do I do besides "grin and bear it" on days I may not be feeling so good when I'm running?

A: Don Glover, a track and cross-country coach at Mariner High School in White Bear Lake, Minnesota, tries to teach his runners the benefits of maintaining a rhythm while running. He feels it is important when you are feeling good, as well as for your down moments.

Running is a rhythmic activity, and Glover tries to teach this to his runners through a word game. First he has them coordinate their breathing pattern with their stride. When their foot hits the ground, they should be exhaling on each stride, or every second step should be accompanied by an outward breath. The pattern depends on the individual. To emphasize this rhythm, he adds the phrase "I can do it" to a four-part harmony with the foot plant and the breathing. Land, exhale, and think "I"; land, exhale, and think "can"; repeat and think "do"; repeat and think "it." To quicken the cadence, you shorten the phrase to "can do it" and finally to "do it."

Find your own system for maintaining a rhythm. When you are running rhythmically, you'll notice the difference from when you are running in a tired, nonrhythmic gait. Your body seems to glide when everything is working together, and maintaining a rhythm is one way to blend all the parts together into a smooth unit.

Q: How do you handle dogs when you're running?

A: Most dogs are just defending their territory or property. They don't want to attack you or grab a piece of your leg as a hunting trophy. They are probably afraid of you.

They bark to scare you off, to cause you to retreat. A runner receives much of the dog's abuse because running is regarded as a sign of fear by the dog. To stop the dog's advance, you should face the dog and move aggressively toward it. Be menacing and the dog will usually retreat. If the dog continues its charge, grab a weapon and defend yourself. Carry a spray can with ammonia water in it and aim for the nose of the attacking animal. This should stop the attack.

Q: Is 40 too late to start a running program?

A: It is never too late to start. You just have to be more

careful when you begin. Anyone who starts running at an advanced age should be especially careful to get checked out by a physiologist or physician before starting a running program.

Forty-four-year-old Jack Foster of New Zealand is one of the best marathon runners in the world, and forty two-year-old Miki Gorman ran the fastest time in the world for women in that event in her forty-first year. Both of these people started running after their thirtieth birthday. They were in good shape before they began and are exceptional physical specimens. You probably won't be setting world records, but you'll improve your condition and your chances for a longer, healthier life through exercise.

Q: Is there any danger to health from running in the rain?

A: Only that you might slip on a wet surface and fall. It is not wise to run in thunderstorms because of the danger of lightning, but a normal rain shower can only get you wet, not cause any permanent damage. You should wear light-weight clothes so that you don't soak up a lot of water. A nylon rain suit is best for colder days, with shorts and a turtleneck underneath. Shoes with softer, more absorbent rubber soles improve traction, but this is only important to racers.

Q: Does it hurt a youngster to start running early in life?

A: No, the only danger is doing too much too soon. If too many expectations are placed on a youngster early in life, it could lead to his rejecting the activity because of fear of failure or loss of interest. Many times a parent or coach will notice talent in a young person and try to develop or exploit that talent too early. Most children do not want to be regimented or locked into a daily training routine at an early age. Variety and activity are fine, but specific training for distance running usually hurts more than it helps. For every child prodigy in distance running, there is usually a burned-out runner by the time the individual reaches college.

Steve Prefontaine, one of America's great distance runners, ran a national record for the two-mile in high school on a very light training regimen. He improved throughout his career as his work load increased and never lost the zest for competition or running.

The old adage "It is better to undertrain than overtrain" applies doubly to youngsters. Physical activity is good, but too much can leave mental scars that may never be repaired.

Q: Is it better to run on a track or off a track while training?

A: The track is for specific activity, timed running. If you want an exact time for a specific distance, the track is the place to go. Most of your running can be done out on the roads, fields, and paths rather than round and round on a track. Racers use tracks sparingly to sharpen their speed and increase confidence. Runners can use them if they are curious about how fast they can run for a set distance, but for everyday training they tend to be boring.

The curves of a track can also put added stress on your ankles and legs. If you do run some distance on a track, it is good to change direction occasionally to help counteract this problem.

Q: Is one surface better than another for running?

A: On the track a tartan or chevron material is best because it absorbs the impact better. Rubberized asphalt tracks tend to harden in cold weather and are harder on your legs than the softer tartan surfaces. Roads tend to be harder on your legs than grass or dirt trails, but you adapt to it. The smooth surface of the road keeps sprained ankles at a minimum, while uneven, grassy surfaces can be more dangerous. No one surface is the best. You will adapt to any surface.

Q: Where can I get up-to-date information on running?

A: *Runner's World,* a publication based in California, is a monthly magazine offering information on running. To subscribe, you can write to Box 2680, Boulder, Colorado 80302. The cost is $9.50 for 12 issues.

You could also try to find local distance running clubs. They are flourishing all over the country and are generally run by people like you who want to share their experiences with others. The Road Runners Club of America and the National Jogging Association, both mentioned in the previous chapter, are also good sources of information.

More and more sporting-goods stores are being started by runners, and this is another good source of information and equipment. Phidippides and Athletic Attic in the South, Bill Rodgers' Running Shop in Massachusetts, Frank Shorter Sports in Colorado and Michigan, and Running World and Body n' Sole in Minnesota are some of the shops that specialize in serving the needs of the runner.

Index